VITAL TO EARTH!
Keystone Species Explained

T0012409

GRAY WOLVES

IN THEIR ECOSYSTEMS

by Della O'Dowd

BEARPORT
PUBLISHING

Minneapolis, Minnesota

Credits
Cover and title page, © jimcumming88/Adobe Stock; 4–5, © Petr Bonek/Alamy; 7, © Michal Martinek/Shutterstock; 8–9, © Donald M. Jones/Minden; 10–11, © Sam Brockway/500px/Getty; 12–13, © Gerald Corsi/iStock; 15, © FastGlassPhotos/iStock; 16–17, © Michael Wheatley/Alamy; 18, © Banu R/iStock; 18–19, © American Wildlife Institute/Public Domain; 20–21, © American art/Alamy; 22–23, © LIONEL CIRONNEAU/AP; 24–25, © Michael Roeder/iStock; 26–27, © Design Pics Inc/Alamy; 28, © Byrdyak/iStock; 29T, © Luke23/Shutterstock; 29TM, © Michael Roeder/iStock; 29M, © Jeffrey Whyte/Alamy; 29BM, © Jim Mone/AP; 29B, © PeopleImages/iStock.

Bearport Publishing Company Product Development Team
President: Jen Jenson; Director of Product Development: Spencer Brinker; Managing Editor: Allison Juda; Associate Editor: Naomi Reich; Associate Editor: Tiana Tran; Art Director: Colin O'Dea; Designer: Elena Klinkner; Designer: Kayla Eggert; Product Development Assistant: Owen Hamlin

STATEMENT ON USAGE OF GENERATIVE ARTIFICIAL INTELLIGENCE
Bearport Publishing remains committed to publishing high-quality nonfiction books. Therefore, we restrict the use of generative AI to ensure accuracy of all text and visual components pertaining to a book's subject. See BearportPublishing.com for details.

Library of Congress Cataloging-in-Publication Data

Names: O'Dowd, Della, author.
Title: Gray wolves in their ecosystems / by Della O'Dowd.
Description: Minneapolis, Minnesota : Bearport Publishing Company, [2024] |
   Series: Vital to earth! Keystone species explained | Includes
   bibliographical references and index.
Identifiers: LCCN 2023039775 (print) | LCCN 2023039776 (ebook) | ISBN
   9798889166283 (library binding) | ISBN 9798889166351 (paperback) | ISBN
   9798889166412 (ebook)
Subjects: LCSH: Gray wolf--Reintroduction--Yellowstone National
   Park--Juvenile literature. | Gray wolf--Conservation--Juvenile
   literature.
Classification: LCC QL737.C22 O36 2024 (print) | LCC QL737.C22 (ebook) |
   DDC 599.77309787/52--dc23/eng/20230907
LC record available at https://lccn.loc.gov/2023039775
LC ebook record available at https://lccn.loc.gov/2023039776

For more information, write to Bearport Publishing, 5357 Penn Avenue South, Minneapolis, MN 55419.

Contents

The Wild Wolf

The sun shines over a green forest. Birds flit from branch to branch, and fish leap out of the river to catch insects. Nearby, a beaver repairs its dam, and young, healthy elk **graze** as they make their way through the trees. This forest is bursting with activity.

It may seem odd, but all this life is made possible by a pack of animals usually linked with death— gray wolves. These amazing **predators** are vital to their **ecosystems**!

For almost a million years, gray wolves have roamed North America, Europe, and Asia. There are several kinds of gray wolves as well as another **species** of wolves called the Ethiopian wolf.

A Key Animal

Gray wolves are a keystone species—a kind of plant or animal that is crucial to supporting an entire community of life within an area. These species shape the land or help balance the populations of its plants and animals in a way that benefits everything in the environment.

As **apex predators**, gray wolves control who lives and dies. When wolves kill **prey**, it has an effect throughout the ecosystem. The plants or animals the prey would eat now have a chance to survive.

Gray wolves are powerful mammals that hold the top predator spot in many different habitats. Gray wolves can make their homes in forests, grasslands, **tundra**, and deserts.

Gray wolves are the largest members of the canine family.

The Big Dogs

Gray wolves hunt huge grazing animals, including elk, moose, and bison. These natural-born killers use their size, speed, and very sharp teeth to take down prey. But their real strength comes from working together. Gray wolves can kill animals much larger than themselves by hunting as a pack.

Wolf packs are smart hunters. They pick the oldest or weakest members of a herd to attack. This may sound cruel, but it improves the whole herd's long-term chances. A younger, stronger herd is more likely to stay healthy.

Wolves can eat 20 pounds (9 kg) of meat at a time! And they have no problem sharing. After they've had their fill, wolves leave their leftovers for other **carnivores**.

Greedy Grazers

Grazing animals, such as elk and bison, live on grasslands in large herds. If a herd eats too much **vegetation** in one area, the land may dry out. When heavy rain falls, the area may flood without the roots of plants to soak up extra water.

Plants do more than feed grazers. They provide food and shelter to plant-eating birds, mice, turtles, muskrats, and even bears. **Overgrazing** impacts all these other animals in an ecosystem.

How do wolves help prevent this overgrazing? In areas where gray wolves live, grazing animals are always on the lookout. To stay safe, the herds don't stay in one place very long. This allows time for the plants and trees to grow back, keeping the habitat healthy.

Keep It Moving!

Which plants grazers eat—or don't eat—along the rivers and streams in the forest is just as important as how much. Large grazers often munch on young trees that grow in these habitats. But if the trees are gobbled up before they get big, all forest life suffers.

When gray wolves keep the forest's grazers on the move, many young trees are left alone. Then, the trees can grow tall and leafy, providing food and shelter to small animals. Trees that shade rivers and streams create a cool place for young fish to grow.

Saving trees also helps another keystone species—the beaver. Beavers use tree branches to build dams that create ponds bursting with plant and animal life.

Moose often eat young trees growing near water.

Control the Coyotes

In addition to keeping grazers on the move, wolves in an area help with other threats to the habitat. Without wolves around, coyotes take over. These smaller canine relatives don't leave leftovers after their feasts. This makes it harder for **scavengers** to find a meal.

Coyotes typically eat most of the smaller animals in a habitat. They may hunt and gobble up all the mice, rabbits, squirrels, beavers, fish, and birds in the ecosystem. Other animals that also rely on these creatures for food can't compete with the coyotes. They may even starve to death.

Coyotes don't hunt large grazers. When coyotes take over an area, grazers often stay put for longer, eating too much vegetation and leaving little behind for the other creatures that rely on the plants.

A coyote having a meal

Learning from the Gray Wolf

Many Native American communities have long respected how gray wolves protect their shared ecosystems. They have lived alongside these keystone species for years, and have incorporated stories about the creatures into their cultures. The Blackfoot, Lakota, and Cheyenne peoples even claim to have modeled their hunting parties on the wolf pack, with groups working as one.

In Squamish art and teachings, the wolf is a symbol for leadership.

Because of wolves' importance and intelligence, some Cherokee peoples refuse to harm the animals. Those Native American communities that hunt wolves do so very carefully to be sure to keep enough of the keystone species around.

Killing the Wolf

Europeans and European settlers in North America saw gray wolves differently. They killed wolves out of fear over the safety of their **livestock** and families. Europeans began killing wolves in large numbers.

Gray wolves were hunted to **extinction** across many parts of Europe. In North America, the spread of farms and ranches put the wolves in deadly conflict with settlers, seriously threatening the survival of the species. The creatures became **endangered**.

In the 1800s, the American bison was almost wiped out by over-hunting. Losing this important food source pushed the gray wolves in North America even closer to extinction.

The government paid some people to kill gray wolves. People made money by selling wolf skins, too.

A Land without Life

Ecosystems suffered from the loss of gray wolf populations. Without this keystone species, the damage quickly became clear in places like Yellowstone National Park.

By 1926, there were no gray wolves left in the park. As a result, the number of elk exploded. Because they could now safely graze in one place for longer, the elk ate many young trees before they could grow tall. Soon, birds, fish, and beavers disappeared. Without wolf kills, scavengers went hungry. The park's ecosystem began to collapse.

When beavers left Yellowstone, their dams fell apart and the beavers' ponds washed away, leaving dry, empty land behind. All the animal and plant life around the beaver ponds was gone.

Yellowstone National Park in 1902

Welcome Home, Wolves!

People realized something had to be done to restore the balance between predators and prey in Yellowstone. Only then would the area's plant and animal community come back healthy.

Beginning in 1995, park officials began **reintroducing** wolves into Yellowstone. They brought more than 40 Canadian wolves to the park by plane, truck, and even mule wagon! To get used to their new home, the wolves spent the first few weeks in large open-air pens within the park.

Dead elk were hidden in the wolf pens at Yellowstone. This gave the wolves a chance to get used to their new environment and develop a taste for the prey.

Scientists carefully released gray wolves in Yellowstone.

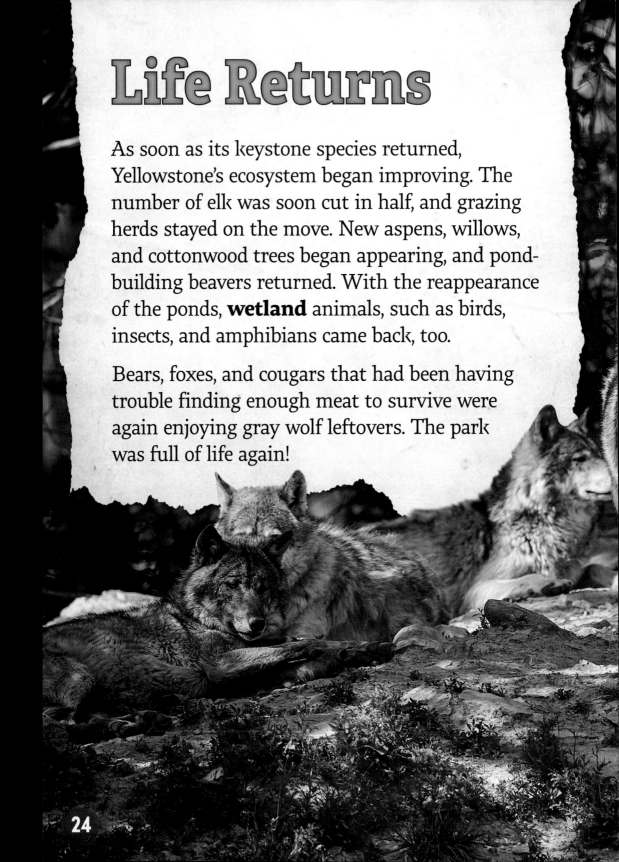

Life Returns

As soon as its keystone species returned, Yellowstone's ecosystem began improving. The number of elk was soon cut in half, and grazing herds stayed on the move. New aspens, willows, and cottonwood trees began appearing, and pond-building beavers returned. With the reappearance of the ponds, **wetland** animals, such as birds, insects, and amphibians came back, too.

Bears, foxes, and cougars that had been having trouble finding enough meat to survive were again enjoying gray wolf leftovers. The park was full of life again!

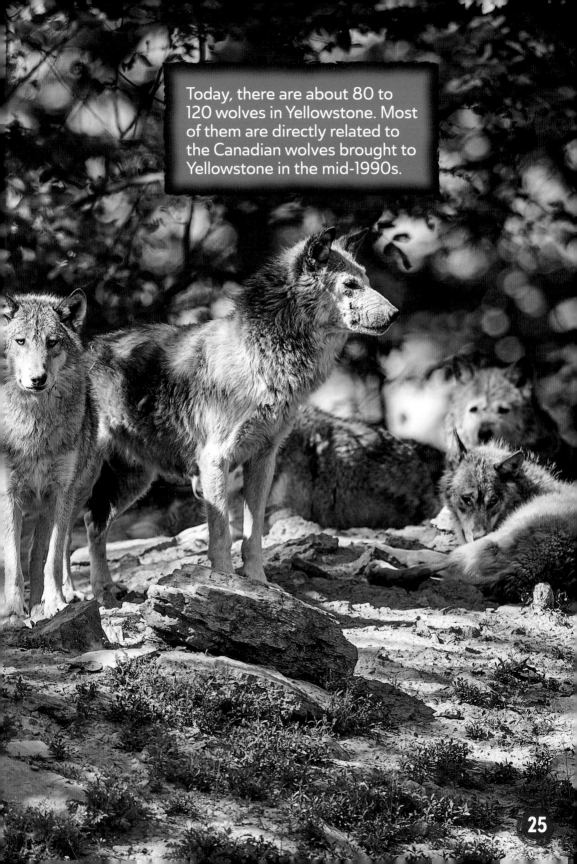

Today, there are about 80 to 120 wolves in Yellowstone. Most of them are directly related to the Canadian wolves brought to Yellowstone in the mid-1990s.

Protecting the Protectors

Though many people changed their minds about gray wolves after seeing their impact on Yellowstone, wolves still need our help. Today, government programs are helping keep gray wolves safe. Wolf reintroduction is underway throughout Mexico, the United States, and Canada. Nature experts teach people why these wolves that protect their ecosystems must also be protected.

It's clear how important gray wolves are. They're not just predators—they're a keystone species. When gray wolves thrive, their ecosystems stay in balance.

Gray wolves were once found in every state except Hawaii. In the United States today, wolves live in only about a dozen states.

Save the Gray Wolves

Because gray wolves are so important to the health and well-being of life on our planet, when they are in danger, we all are. Luckily, there are some easy things we can do to protect this keystone species and help it in its life-giving work.

Tell people about the good things gray wolves do for nature. These hunters are also helpers!

Fight for the continued safety of animals in parks, including Yellowstone. Animals need protected wild areas to live even more desperately as humans take over more of their homelands.

Visit, support, or volunteer for a wolf rehabilitation center.

Support organizations, politicians, and programs fighting to protect wolves.

Talk to farmers and ranchers about how to keep livestock safe without killing wolves. Electric fences, guard dogs, and scare devices are all non-deadly ways to keep wolves away from farm animals.

Glossary

apex predators animals that are not hunted by any other animals

carnivores animals that eat meat

ecosystems communities of animals and plants that depend on one another to live

endangered close to dying off completely

extinction when a type of plant or animal dies out completely

graze to eat grass; animals that primarily eat grass are called grazers

livestock animals, such as horses, sheep, and cows, that are raised on farms or ranches

overgrazing eating in an area to the point of damaging the vegetation

predators animals that hunt and eat other animals

prey animals that are hunted by other animals for food

reintroducing bringing animals back into an area where they once lived

scavengers animals that feed on the dead bodies of other animals

species groups that plants and animals are divided into, according to similar characteristics

tundra cold, treeless land where the ground is frozen just below the surface

vegetation plant life

wetland an area of land where the soil is usually covered by shallow water

Read More

Cooke, Tim. *Return to Yellowstone: Gray Wolf Comeback (Saving Animals from the Brink).* Minneapolis: Bearport Publishing, 2022.

Isabella, Jude. *Bringing Back the Wolves: How a Predator Restored an Ecosystem.* Toronto, ON: Kids Can Press, 2020.

Kenney, Karen Latchana. *Wolf Pack (Better Together: Animal Groups).* Minneapolis: Jump!, Inc., 2020.

Learn More Online

1. Go to **www.factsurfer.com** or scan the QR code below.

2. Enter "**Keystone Gray Wolves**" into the search box.

3. Click on the cover of this book to see a list of websites.

Index

About the Author

Della O'Dowd is a writer with a passion for nature. When she's not writing, she's hiking, drawing, or going on an adventure with her dog. It's her dream to visit every national park someday.